A Beginner's Guide to Pendulum Dowsing

Unravelling the Mystery

Brenda Hunt

What is dowsing?

Everyone has heard of dowsing for water with a forked twig or two rods.

It's what people used to do, isn't it? In the olden days – before we learnt that you couldn't just find water with twigs!

But some people could find a water supply by dowsing for it, people still can, and the power of dowsing isn't restricted to locating underground water.

Dowsing is used to find water and minerals, it is also used to find lost objects, people or pets, for divination and decision making, for medical diagnosis and for healing. It can be used in your personal, everyday life as well as by professional dowsers working for governments and large corporations.

In fact it's a fascinating world, which most of us know nothing about in our modern, technological lives. But there's no reason for that to remain the case.

This book is designed to introduce you to the craft or art of dowsing.

It can guide you along the way in your journey to new and exciting knowledge.

It will teach you the basic techniques of dowsing that you need to begin with. It will go on to show you some more advanced ones that you can develop as you become more comfortable with your pendulum and more experienced.

It will also give you some ideas about how to work with your pendulum and the areas of life where dowsing can be helpful once you master the basic techniques.

But once you have learnt the techniques and the possibilities, the only true way to learn how you can dowse is to do it!

Open up your mind and your senses and enter into this fascinating world.

The History of Dowsing

Dowsing is a human skill that is as old as human history. There are cave drawings that can be seen as early man dowsing – probably for water. One, found in Algeria, of a man holding a forked stick, has been dated to 6000BC.

The Chinese and ancient Egyptians are also part of the history of dowsing, with dowsers appearing on a statue of a Chinese emperor from about 2200BC, and in Egyptian paintings and papyri.

The publication of De Re Metallica by Agricola in  the 1550's is the earliest known illustration of a dowser in literature. It was a work on mining and metallurgy and shows the man using a forked twig in searching for mineral veins.

France has been one of the strongholds of information on dowsing. The work of priests such as the Abbe de Vallmont in the seventeenth century came despite the fact that the Church condemned dowsing for divination as early as 1326.

Throughout the ages dowsing has remained an important human skill, each new age using it for their own ends, whether searching for water, minerals or answers.

It travelled with settlers as they moved around the world to the Americas, across Africa and to Australia. It became the source of experimentation - in the 1750's they looked for a connection between dowsing and electricity, a theory still popular today. The Academie des Sciences in France set up a commission to explore the use of the rod in 1853.

A change in attitudes

Until Victorian times, dowsing was a natural art, taken for granted, accepted and even respected, certainly not doubted.

But the Industrial Revolution, the move of populations from the country to the town, the growth of industrial systems, the worship of the sciences and the growth of urban life finally managed to marginalise dowsing along with many other skills such as herbal medicine and healing skills. So it became a rural art, one often used by children before they grew too old and realised that 'it couldn't possibly work!'

In more recent years, as we've learnt that not everything can be proven in a laboratory, dowsing has been gaining in popularity once more.

Again French priests were at the forefront of the dowsing movement at the beginning of the nineteenth century.

Abbe Bouly, a priest from a French village on the coast of the English Channel, worked with French and other European manufacturers to find water sources. After the First World War, he worked to find unexploded shells in the ravaged ground, apparently being able to tell the difference between German and Allied shells before they were unearthed. His work led to him being recommended to the Ministry of War in Paris.

He coined the term *radiesthaesia* to describe the use of the pendulum in dowsing. He used the Latin term *radius* for radiation and the Greek word *eshaesis* meaning sensitivity.

His work on dowsing continued throughout his life. He did experimental work with various hospitals including Lille and Liege where he was able to use a dowsing pendulum to identify different microbe cultures in test tubes and was able to repeat the results as accurately as if he were working with a microscope.

In his eighties in 1950, he was awarded the highest decoration France could give; he was made a Chevalier de La Legion d'Honneur.

In his acceptance speech he said '.....this is awarded in my person to all practitioners of dowsing.'

Together with another priest, the Abbe Mermet, Bouley organised a series of congresses to research the many uses of dowsing, especially with a pendulum. They concentrated especially on the use in health and medical areas.

Mermet is considered by many to be the most famous pendulum expert that ever lived and his use of the pendulum covered many areas, from finding lost children to helping solve archaeological enigmas for the Vatican.

His book entitled *How I Proceed in the Discovery of Near or Distant Water, Metals, Hidden Objects and Illnesses,* is considered a classic. He also claimed that he invented the method of pendulum diagnosis.

Abbe Mermet had learnt to dowse from his grandfather and he worked with another priest, Father Bourdoux who, as a missionary in Brazil for many years, had been treated by his parishioners with local plant medicine when he had been suffering from consumption and then later, a long fever.

After many years of study, including another visit to South America he published his book *Practical Notions of Radiesthesia for Missionaries.*

In the preface he wrote:

'If you have the patience to read these pages you shall see how, thanks to the new science called 'radiesthesia,' you will be able, without any medical training and hardly any funds, to succour both believers and pagans. Perhaps you will be amazed at some of the things I have set down and be tempted to say, "That's impossible." But are we not living in a time of marvellous discoveries each more disconcerting than the next?'

3

Dowsing today

Today, the pendulum has become the tool of choice for many professional dowsers.

Again, in France, Andre Bovis invented techniques for gauging the freshness and quality of foods using a pendulum. And on a more personal level, it is a very useful way to test if certain foods or supplements are right for you.

But research hasn't been limited to France. At the Rockefeller Institute in New York, Dr Alexis Carrel – the Nobel Prize winner – decided that the whole person must be treated in an illness and that, in his opinion, radiesthaesia deserved serious consideration in the treatment of patients. Indeed, in France, many doctors use the pendulum as one of their tools for diagnostic and therapeutic uses.

The publication of a book in 1922 by Dr Albert Abrams, an English physician, describing the use of a pendulum for diagnostic, medical and therapeutic purposes, encouraged the growth of pendulum use in America.

During World War Two, General Patton used dowsers to find underground water supplies and they were used again to find underground tunnels and booby traps during the Vietnam War.

During the 1960's the American dowser Verne Cameron was considered a security risk by the CIA and the US government after he successfully located every US and Soviet submarine on a map of the Pacific using his pendulum. When the South African government invited him to visit, to help them locate precious natural resources, the US government would not allow him to leave the country, refusing him a passport and stating that he was a risk to national security.

You can find many official accounts of the successes of dowsing.

For instance the Daily Telegraph in 1994 printed the following obituary:

"Colonel Kenneth Merrylees, the water-diviner who has died aged 97, worked during the Second World War as a bomb-disposal expert, when he used his dowsing skills to find bombs with delayed-action fuses which had penetrated deep into the ground."

The future?
Dowsing societies have grown up all over the world during the 20th century. Britain has over 20 while America has over 70 chapters affiliated to the American Society of Dowsers. In the Soviet Union it

was even possible to take a masters degree in dowsing – termed the 'bioplasmic method'.

Today, dowsing is accepted by UNESCO, major corporations and the Canadian ministry of Agriculture.

In 1897 Sir JJ Thomson discovered the electron which has enabled the technology we take for granted from TV's to computers, a discovery for which he was knighted and given the Nobel Prize. When speaking to a group of eminent scientists, he requested that they should give their attention to the physics of dowsing. So far this has fallen on deaf ears, but all over the world people have discovered for themselves the opportunities opened up by dowsing.

Remember, the mind is like a parachute

– it works best when it is open.

4

Why should it work?

Often, the first reaction to the unknown is to be sceptical.

How does it work?

Why does it work?

It can't possibly work, it's all rubbish!

That is often the path that our 'modern' minds take.

But in the 21st century, many of us are becoming more open once more, and willing to explore other possibilities and other ways of looking at the world.

Eastern philosophy and medicine has always accepted that we are beings of energy as well as solid physical mass, and western science is beginning to accept this as well.

We accept easily that some energies are very destructive to us, even fatal. We accept that medical X rays should be used in moderation and that those operating the equipment should be protected with lead. We accept that lasers can be used to destroy parts of us that are harming or disfiguring the whole.

Now think more personally. The human senses or sensitivity often gives warning signals which we tend to ignore. We call it intuition, feelings, bad vibes. Whatever you want to call it, or however you choose to dismiss it, our energy field is constantly interacting with the energy around us. When we meet new people we can feel instantly drawn to them or uncomfortable and we look for logical reasons, ignoring the feeling – often at our peril – if we can't locate 'real' reasons.

Places, situations, decisions, even directions when you're driving can give signals to your senses. If I take a wrong turn on a journey, even when I've never been to that area before, I know I'm going the wrong way. I 'feel' uncomfortable. It can make ring roads and detours difficult, but I've learnt to listen to that sensory message, it can save a lot of petrol and time.

Once you begin to listen to your inner voice, to accept that the senses that pick up energy signals are as valid as those that tell you what colour you are seeing or if the saucepan you are reaching out for is too hot to touch, you will learn to tune into them more naturally and your use of the pendulum will become more accurate and more natural.

There have been many attempts to explain how dowsing works, but whatever you decide for yourself – electricity, radar, the subconscious – the basic bottom line is that it is energy and it works.

Edison was asked, "What is electricity?" His reply – "I don't know what it is, but it's there, let's use it."

5

Choosing your pendulum

Although very modern in comparison with rods, the pendulum has become a very popular tool for dowsing, especially among professional dowsers. Some dowsers do still prefer to work with the traditional rods, but a pendulum is convenient to carry and to use, especially when dowsing for health, where accuracy in a very small area is important.

It is also a very convenient method when you want to be able to react quickly, much easier to take a pendulum out of your pocket or bag them to carry your dowsing rods at all times.

At its simplest, a pendulum is a small, weighted object suspended from a chain or string which you can hold lightly between the thumb and forefinger, allowing the weight to swing freely. In an emergency you can create a pendulum from a piece of string and a key!

In general, though, I find it much better to work with a pendulum that is well balanced and is tuned to you.

You can buy pendulums that follow the design used by Abbe Mermet, a metal weight with a compartment within it. You place an item that is relevant to the purpose of your dowsing in the compartment. For instance, if you were searching for a lost pet, you could place a piece of that pet's fur in the space.

Other pendulums are made from metal, glass or wood. Personally I am drawn to the healing energies of crystals, so it's not surprising that I prefer pendulums made from gemstones , especially quartz, such as clear quartz, amethyst (purple) or rose quartz (pink).

The most important thing is that you feel 'comfortable' with your pendulum. It should feel physically comfortable in your hand, not too heavy - some pendulum designs are quite large, and not too small - you want it to have enough weight to work for you.

The chain or cord should be comfortable as well. It has to rest gently between your thumb and forefinger, not held tightly or wrapped around your hand. The pendulum should be doing the work, not your hand. So the chain or cord should be a comfortable length for you. Some have beads at the top, some rings, and some no specific end at all. Choose what you prefer.

If you are buying in person, try the different pendulums on offer and get the feel of each. Very often, a pendulum will just feel right in your hand. If the people in the shop or at a stall don't allow you to try the pendulum or the atmosphere makes you feel uncomfortable, walk away. Any crystals, including pendulums in that kind of atmosphere will have absorbed negative energy. So just leave them unless you're feeling strongly drawn to a specific pendulum.

Of course, nowadays many purchases are made online, and I feel that you can get a true, almost a purer reaction to a crystal pendulum in that way. After all, there is nothing else to distract you, such as the atmosphere of the shop, the scent of incense or the colour of the surroundings. Many of my favourite pieces have come to me over the Internet and often over many thousands of miles.

One pendulum or many?

You may find that you feel comfortable using different pendulums for different types of dowsing.

I have quite a number, some that I just couldn't resist when I saw them. They are different designs, gemstones and sizes.

I like to use a clear quartz for dowsing for physical health problems and energy fields. It's the one I carry around with me all the time and will use on a daily basis. It's with me if I feel I need to check the energy of food in the supermarket or the energy in an area, or the many other times the dowsing pendulum is useful in daily life, as you will discover as you read the following pages.

I also tend to work with a rose quartz or amethyst when it concerns emotional or spiritual questions. The rose quartz is an excellent crystal energy for emotional matters including love, self-confidence and creativity, and personally I find the crystal energy adds to the dowsing when the questions are in that specific energy area. In the same way amethyst is a wonderful crystal energy when dealing with spiritual or psychic energies.

But I also have other pendulums of rarer crystals such as astrophyllite, black tourmaline and lapis lazuli, which I work with when I feel that I need to involve that crystal energy.

Choosing your pendulum, whether you want one or many is a personal matter.

Does it feel physically comfortable?

Are you drawn to it - still thinking about it when you leave the shop?

Is it the first one you look at and keep going back to?

Dowse with the pendulum, asking it if it is the right one for you or if it is the right one for the purpose you have in mind.

Are you looking for a specific design or crystal?

If you work with healing crystals, and so are used to choosing crystals, you can use the same techniques – whatever personal techniques you use - for choosing your pendulum, especially for crystal pendulums.

If you already have a pendulum, you can dowse about choosing another one, dowsing over the pendulum in question if you want to, or dowsing about a pendulum choice when you're purchasing online.

Intuition is very important!

As with all types of energy work, using your intuition, listening to your inner voices and following your feelings are very important.

Strengthening your intuition and learning to listen to the messages it is sending to you, is one of the most important parts of learning to be successful with dowsing, so choosing your pendulum is a good place to start practicing.

How do you know which pendulum to go for?

Literally – which one attracts your attention? You just 'want' to be with it.

A crystal or pendulum can make you feel good just by looking at it, just by holding it for a moment. They can bring joy, a sense of well being and peace.

But don't think that it's going to be spectacular. You're not waiting for fireworks or a virtual neon sign pointing to a particular pendulum, the signs can be subtle. So if you find yourself thinking that one of them is a lovely colour, looks more balanced in shape or it just attracts your attention, listen to the signs. You'll get better at reading the signs and learning to recognise the message that your intuition is sending you – listening to your gut reaction.

There are also some general guidelines on actually choosing the individual dowsing pendulum.

Try to make sure that you are calm and open when you choose a pendulum to work with. You may like to take a deep breath and release it slowly, mentally clearing out negative thoughts as you release the breath.

You want to be physically comfortable so that you are not distracted. Try to wear comfortable clothing and footwear and don't weigh yourself down with heavy bags.

Try and give yourself space. Wait until people have moved away or try and move into an empty space yourself.

You also want time. It's not a good idea to choose anything when you're feeling rushed and hassled, especially if other people are pressuring you on time or decision making.

If you are looking for a pendulum for a specific purpose, keep that purpose in mind as you make your selection.

You are 'feeling' the energy of the crystal or pendulum as you choose it. How you actually sense that, differs with different people.

You may 'see' it, in which case you choose by looking, picking the pendulum which attracts you. You can do this by closing your eyes, taking your deep breath, concentrating on your purpose, then opening your eyes and picking up the first one you see. This can also happen when there isn't a selection for you to choose from. You can just come across a single pendulum and just know that you have to have it!

You may literally 'feel' it when you touch a pendulum. It could grow warm or cold, make your hand tingle or just call out to be picked up. You can do this by picking up each one in turn until you find one that 'feels' right.

Alternatively you can place a selection of pendulums in front of you – you can ask someone else to do this so that your eyes can't guide you in memory – close your eyes and let your hand pass over the selection. Keep doing this until you feel drawn to pick up the pendulum under your hand.

If you already dowse and have a pendulum, of course you can dowse for the answer. You can either ask your own pendulum if the new one is right for you and your purpose, or you can dowse over a selection until your pendulum picks out a new one for you.

You can also dowse with the prospective new pendulum. Pick it up and first of all, ask it to show you its 'yes' and 'no' answers. (see chapter 6) Once you have a clear picture of what it is saying to you, ask it if it is the right piece for you – some will say no!

6

Programming your pendulum

Before you can work with a dowsing pendulum, you have to know what it is telling you when it moves.

A dowsing pendulum works by giving you responses to a clear question. The standard possible answers are 'Yes', 'No' and 'Neutral' although you can develop the range of other answers that your pendulum can show as you become more comfortable with dowsing.

Dowsing rods respond to the presence of water or other items you are looking for by moving from sitting parallel from your hands to crossing one another.

A dowsing pendulum will react as it swings from the chain or cord it is hanging from as you hold it.

There are only certain ways that a weight on the end of a cord can move – in circles, backwards and forwards or by vibrating.

A pendulum can of course make any of these movements, so you have to be able to tell what movement in your pendulum indicates a 'neutral' or 'don't know' response, which is the 'yes' or 'positive' response and which is the 'no' or 'negative' response.

There are basically two ways to programme a new pendulum, either you tell it what you want it to do, forcing it into a certain pattern, or you let the pendulum show you what its answers are.

Personally, I prefer the second method, working with the pendulum, especially as I tend to work with crystal pendulums and I like to work with the energy of crystals rather than mould them into a pattern.

Before you begin either way of programming, you should get comfortable with your pendulum first. You can do this by carrying it with you for a while, making sure that it is protected from scratches by wrapping it in a soft cloth or placing it in a small bag or pouch.

You can also hold it while you are relaxing or meditating, allowing your mind to clear. Listening to calming music might help or sitting comfortably in a quiet room with gently scented candles. There really isn't a right or wrong way to relax, just find a way that works for you.

Once you feel that you are in tune with your new pendulum, you can begin the programming process.

Again, there isn't a right or wrong answer as to how long this will take.

Children attune very quickly, sometimes almost as soon as they pick up a pendulum. But the older we get, the more entrenched we become in our modern, scientific and closed way of looking at the world. So don't worry if it takes you a few days, or even a few weeks before you become comfortable and the pendulum begins to work with you.

If you begin the programming procedure and the pendulum doesn't really do anything at all, just relax, stay calm and put it back in the bag and carry it with you for another little while and try again.

The more you work with dowsing pendulums, the more quickly you will be able to programme a new one until it becomes an almost instant process.

What movements can a pendulum show?

Obviously, there are a limited number of ways in which a pendulum can move, so what sort of patterns should you expect?

There is a Circular clockwise movement

A Circular anti-clockwise movement

A left to right movement – across your body line

A backwards and forwards movement – away from and towards your body line

And a diagonal movement, either top left/bottom right or top right/bottom left.

Finally, the pendulum can also hang still or vibrate gently on its chain or string.

Active programming

In this method you programme the pendulum to match the indicator of your choice to the answer rather than letting the pendulum show you its own indicator.

You must be able to focus your thoughts very clearly when you use this method, as you are focusing your intention into the pendulum and that intention has to be very clear.

Remember to be polite, making sure that your thoughts are peaceful and loving. You are still asking a pendulum to work with you, not demanding that it does as you tell it.

Prepare yourself before you begin

Calm your thoughts and empty your mind of negative energies. Remember, as with anything you do, negative emotions or energies will interfere with your pendulum dowsing.

- Take a deep breath and let it out slowly.
- Sit comfortably, but do not cross your feet, you don't want to enclose your energy.
- Hold the pendulum between the thumb and forefinger of your dominant hand, letting your wrist relax. Hold it securely but lightly – don't grip, just let the chain or cord rest between your fingers so that you don't drop your pendulum.

Programming the 'yes' indicator
- Clear your mind and concentrate on the word 'Yes'. You can say it out loud or mentally.
- Swing the pendulum gently in a clockwise circular pattern while saying 'This is my 'yes' indicator'. Imagine that if you had a pencil on the end of a

piece of string, you would be drawing circles on a piece of paper below the pendulum.

- Although the clockwise/anticlockwise movement is the normal choice, you can choose another movement if you prefer. If you do, make your chosen movement with the pendulum while you concentrate on the word. You can choose whichever movement you are comfortable with (clockwise, anticlockwise, right/left, backwards/forwards) but you must stay with the same movement once you've chosen it.
- Do this for a couple of minutes until you feel that the signal has become linked to the pendulum.
- Repeat this until you are comfortable and until the pendulum makes the chosen movement to the word 'yes' without you forcing it.

You can also ask a question where you know the answer is 'yes' while making the clockwise circles with your pendulum. For instance, *'my name is (your name!)'*

Programming the 'No' indicator

- Swing the pendulum gently in an anti-clockwise circular pattern (or other pattern you have chosen) while saying 'This is my 'No' indicator'. Imagine that if you had a pencil on the end of a piece of string, you would be drawing circles on a piece of paper below the pendulum.

- Do this for a couple of minutes until you feel that the signal has become linked to the pendulum.

You can also ask a question where you know the answer is 'No' while making the anti-clockwise circles with your pendulum. For instance, *'my name is (someone else's name!)'*

Programming a 'neutral' or 'don't know' indicator

This is the movement that your pendulum will make when there isn't a clear 'yes' or 'no'. A pendulum will normally hang still or vibrate gently to give you this indicator, so that is the best thing to do if you want to actively programme a new pendulum

Intuitive programming

For this method you are working with the energy of the dowsing pendulum rather than forcing it into your chosen patterns. I find it a much more comfortable and natural method.

Prepare yourself before you begin

Once you feel ready to begin the programming, make sure that you find somewhere comfortable and quite where you won't be disturbed or distracted

Calm your thoughts and empty your mind of negative energies. Remember, as with anything you do, negative emotions or energies will interfere with your pendulum dowsing.

Make sure that you're comfortable, don't wear clothes that restrict you or feel too tight, too hot or too cold.

Take a deep breath and let it out slowly.

Sit comfortably, but do not cross your feet. Allow your energy field to be open.

Hold the pendulum between the thumb and forefinger of your dominant hand, letting your wrist relax. You are simply holding the pendulum securely so that it won't fall from your hold. You are not gripping it or moving it yourself.

You are working with the dowsing pendulum, so ask it to work with you.

Ask the pendulum to show you its 'neutral' or 'don't know' indicator. Normally the pendulum will hang still or will vibrate gently on the end of its chain or string, but don't force any movement. The idea of this method is to allow the pendulum to show you what indicators it will use. You can ask the question out loud or simply in your mind. Always be polite to your pendulum, you are asking it to work with you, so don't simply demand that it works.

Once you are happy that you know the 'neutral indicator', ask the pendulum to show you its 'yes' answer and wait for a response. The pendulum should start to move, often in a clockwise or anti-clockwise pattern, but sometimes it will be left-right and backwards-forwards. Whatever the pendulum shows you is the 'yes' answer for you with that pendulum. You may find that you have different indicator patterns with different pendulums.

Ask the pendulum to return to its neutral position.

When it has come to its resting position, repeat the process, asking the pendulum to show you its 'no' answer. This will often be the opposite of your 'yes' indicator. Anti-clockwise to a clockwise movement or backwards–forwards to the left-right movement.

The process of programming a dowsing pendulum may be almost immediate or it could take a few days of work, even a couple of weeks before you are really in tune with your pendulum, so don't get despondent.

You may not get the same response with every pendulum, so make sure that you follow the process for each one if you use more than one pendulum.

Even with your regular pendulum, it's worth checking the response sometimes, as it can change temporarily. I always ask mine to show me its basic answers before I start a dowsing session.

Advanced programming

As you do more work, and more detailed work with your pendulum, you will probably find that you require more subtlety in your answers.

So far, you have only asked your pendulum to show you 'yes', 'no' and 'neutral'.

The strength of the answer is reflected in the strength of the movement.

For instance - if your 'yes' indicator is to move clockwise, a small circle will indicate a weak 'positive' or 'yes', while a very large swing will indicate a very strong answer. But there are times when it would be helpful to have more information than this.

It's not a good idea to move on to this stage too quickly. You must be confident in your dowsing ability and your dowsing pendulum before you move on to more advanced work, otherwise you will simply confuse the responses and reduce the efficiency of your dowsing.

Ask your pendulum to show you its indicator for an 'unanswerable question'. Some questions just don't have a clear 'yes' or 'no', and neutral doesn't really tell you that. It's not that there isn't a clear answer, it's more that you've asked a question to which there isn't any answer.

You can also call it the 'stupid' answer because you might be genuinely asking a 'stupid' question!

When you get this response you know that you need to re-phrase your question more carefully or possibly, shouldn't ask that question at all. This happens when you really knew that it wasn't an appropriate question, when you are using the pendulum more as a toy than with a serious intention.

You can also ask the pendulum to show you a 'can't answer' response. This is useful if you have asked a question that literally can't be answered rather than has a neutral or don't know.

This movement will tell you that there may well be an answer, even a clear answer to your question, but for some reason, the pendulum cannot tell you what it is at this time.

My own pendulums have diagonal movements for the 'stupid' and 'can't answer' responses. (one to the left, one to the right).

You probably will not see either of these answers very often, except when you ask your pendulum to show them, and you will not see them at all until you programme the pendulum to give that type of response, but they are very useful when you want to be more detailed in your dowsing work.

It is best to get used to working with your pendulum for a while and to become comfortable with dowsing before you go onto this advanced programming

7

Working with the pendulum

Once you have programmed the pendulum to work with you - what can you do?

The answer to that is simple - practically anything!

People dowse for all sorts of things and reasons. Water is the thing that most of us first connect with dowsing, but you can use a dowsing pendulum in almost any situation where you can ask questions that requires a 'yes' or 'no' - a 'positive' or 'negative' response.

This is a list of some suggestions to get your imagination started, but they are just suggestions. Once you start working with a pendulum, you will quickly find ways in which you can include dowsing in your daily life, both for personal requirements and to help you with work.

You can dowse for small or large reasons,

are those supplements right for me?

should I look for a new career?

The only limit is your imagination.

Dowsing the elements

The most obvious, finding water also known as witching or divining.

Searching for mineral deposits, such as gold, oil or gems and crystals —oil and gas dowsing is quite widely used, but in general oil companies won't admit that they hire dowsers.

Finding water or gas mains or finding leaks.

Choosing crystals for healing

Dowsing for Health

- Dowsing fruit and vegetables for freshness and contaminants – treated, sprayed or irradiated food doesn't have the same strong life force as organic food.

- Testing supplements to check that you require them and that they will suit you.

- Testing for mineral or vitamin deficiencies.

- Body scan to find the problem areas.

- Balancing the Chakra system.

- Distant healing - sending healing vibrations from a distance.

- Removing negative energy from a person's energy field.

- Direct healing over an affected area, very good for easing pain.

o Energizing water and food with positive energy.

Dowsing in the home and garden

- Checking the energy when choosing a new home.
- Checking the use of rooms and placement of furniture.
- Phone book dowsing – finding the best supplier of a product or service for you.
- Garden dowsing to find the best location and soil conditions for particular plants.
- Soil testing to check for mineral deficiencies.
- Tracking down a problem in machines or a car.
- Finding wiring or piping in the wall – before you drill!
- Finding lost objects.

Psychic and Spiritual Dowsing

- Ghost hunting and working with the paranormal.
- Alphabet dowsing.
- Spiritual dowsing - anything connected with finding one's spiritual path
- tracking energy.

- Tracking geopathic zones and electromagnetic fields.
- Transmitting positive Earth energies and warning of negative or over-powerful Earth energies.

The basics of dowsing

Whatever the purpose you chose for your pendulum dowsing, there are certain basic principles for you to learn as you begin to dowse.

It is very important to be clear in your request for your pendulum. The question has to be phrased in a way that can give a 'positive' or 'negative', 'yes' or 'no' answer.

For instance, if you are looking for your car keys it's important to clarify, which keys you are looking for otherwise the pendulum may simply direct you to your house keys. Before you start dowsing, take the time to think clearly about the purpose of your question.

The pendulum is not a toy and dowsing should always be taken seriously. So it's a very good idea to get into the habit of clarifying your thoughts before you start any dowsing.

Preparing to dowse

The basic format for dowsing is the same whatever the purpose. Obviously you will have to adapt some of your methods to deal with surroundings or the actual dowsing that you will be doing, but some of the preparation remains the same.

If possible try to find a quiet space with calm, positive energy, possibly playing soothing music or with scented candles around you.

Try to avoid areas of negative energy or strong electromagnetic energy, unless the presence of these energies are part of your question, for instance,

- can I work in this room, if it is full of electrical equipment?
- or is this house too close to electricity pylons?

If you can't control your physical surroundings, tried to calm your mind and learn how to create your own bubble of tranquillity. Work with whatever energy you are comfortable with. You can say a prayer, ask your Angels to help you, cast a spell or prepare yourself by a period of meditation. Whatever the method you choose, practice it until you can create your own space at will, tuning out the distractions around you and allowing yourself to feel balanced and peaceful. Once you can do this you'll find it a useful ability in many areas of life.

Identify your question and think it through clearly. The question must be clear and precise if you're going to get a useful answer from your dowsing. This will also stop you being too casual with your pendulum. You must remember, it's not a toy, dowsing should be treated seriously and with respect. Once you create the habit of thinking about your questions, you will naturally dismiss any flippant ideas and become more serious about your dowsing.

You might decide that the problem you are going to dowse about will require a series of questions, leading you from the wider picture through to the details that you ultimately require. For instance, if you are trying to make a decision about what path to take in education you may need to narrow it down quite a bit

- Dowse to see if you should continue formal education?
- Dowse to see if you should choose an academic or vocational path?
- Dowse about your area of study?
- Dowse about your choice of college?

Once you have decided on your question or questions, it's always a good idea to ask your pendulum if it is all right to ask this question.

Once you are used to dowsing, you will normally get a positive response to this, because you will have learnt to consider the question before you start, but there are times when the energy is not right to ask a specific question and you'll get a negative response.

If this happens, think about your question and why it might have been given a negative response. Was it a unclear? Was it ambiguous or do you know in your heart that you really shouldn't have asked this question?

In practice a dowsing session will normally follow a pattern such as:

Try to find a peaceful, calm area in which to dowse. If this isn't possible, surround yourself in a bubble of tranquillity.

Calm your mind and clear your thoughts of negative energy.

Sit or stand comfortably, don't cross your legs, you don't want to enclose your energy.

Ask your pendulum if it is all right to ask your questions.

As long as you receive the positive answer to this initial question, continue with your dowsing session, working through your question or list of questions.

Once you have finished, thank your pendulum for its help.

Including dowsing in your daily life.

Although dowsing with your pendulum will become a natural part of your life it should never control your life. It's important not to get into the habit of asking your pendulum for an answer to every question you have. Be sensible. Although it's perfectly reasonable to check with your dowsing pendulum about your food choices in general, you don't need to ask your pendulum if you should have an egg sandwich or a cheese sandwich for lunch!

Once you have become used to your dowsing pendulum it will become a natural part of your daily life, one of the tools that you use naturally.

Most people find that they have an affinity to dowsing in certain areas of their life. For instance, a Reiki healer or a crystal healer will probably use a dowsing pendulum as part of their therapy when treating clients.

I use a dowsing pendulum regularly for helping clear and balance the energy in a clients chakra system and for helping to unwind pain, especially back pain. It's also a very useful tool for helping to pinpoint the source of the pain.

Personally, I work with my pendulums to keep a check on my food choices and the vitamin and herbal supplements I use and well as for checking my decisions making when I feel that I need to, but I don't double check every decision I'm about to make, that would not only be foolish it would damage my ability to follow my instincts and listen to by intuition.

8

Dowsing for Decision making

There are so many decisions that we need to make on a regular basis in our modern complex lives. Some are simple. Some are incredibly complex. Some will have small effects on our lives, others will change them completely.

Obviously, you won't want to resort to your dowsing pendulum to answer every question and every decision that has to be made on a daily basis but used in the proper way dowsing can be a very useful tool in helping us navigate through the modern world.

The dowsing pendulum's ability to give clear 'yes' or 'no' answers to clear questions means that it is a great help when you are trying to make a decision.

This works best when you are genuinely looking for an answer, rather than just trying to reinforce your existing strong opinion or desire, or using the pendulum as a toy – which you should never do!

You must approach the process with an open mind. You might not like the answer that you get, but you must think about it calmly. It would be a great mistake to dismiss an answer out of hand just because it's not the one you were expecting or wanting.

There are many examples where you may need help in focusing your mind and making a decision.

- Choosing a holiday
- choosing between different pieces of healing crystal
- choosing a new home
- choosing a new outfit for an important event
- picking the right college or university
- to do or not to do?
- Deciding whether to make changes in your career
- Deciding if a car is the right one for you
- Deciding which quotation to accept when you're having work done – it's not always as simple as just picking the cheapest

These are just some suggestions to give you an idea of the type and variety of ways that your pendulum can help you in your general life. As you begin to work with it and get more comfortable with dowsing, you will find areas where your pendulum can help you find an answer.

Although the dowsing pendulum can help you in many types of decision-making, in general you probably don't need it to help you between two different pairs of shoes, or which TV programme to watch! Some decisions can be made without the aid of dowsing pendulum.

Once you have decided that you do want to work with your dowsing pendulum on the subject, it's important to decide on your question. That might sound obvious, but you have to phrase your question clearly, and it has to be a question with a definite 'yes', 'no' or 'don't know' answer.

Once you learn to form your questions clearly, it is much easier to get definite answers from your pendulum, so it is worth spending time to focus your thoughts. This will become easier with time and practice.

Many of the more complex decisions in life require a series of questions, and these will help you focus your thoughts about the matter.

However, if you are dowsing to choose between actual objects that are in front of you, you can simply dowse over them, asking if this is the one you should choose for a specific purpose, and allowing the pendulum to tell you 'yes' or 'no'.

Preparing to Dowse

Sit in a quiet space, with a calm, positive energy. You might want to play some soothing music or light some scented candles

If you are going to dowse in a place where you can't control the surroundings – like a shop – try and calm your mind and learn to create your own bubble of tranquillity.

Identify your question. Are you trying to choose for yourself or someone else? Are you choosing the outfit for tonight or as a long term investment? Always be clear about your intention.

Sit or stand comfortably. Don't cross your legs, you don't want to enclose your energy

Relax. Calm and empty your mind of any preconceived opinions or emotions. Take some deep breaths

Ask the pendulum if it is alright for you to begin your questions (you might not always feel the need to do this)

- 'Can I ask this question?'
- 'am I ready?'

As long as you have received the positive indicator for the preparation question, hold the pendulum over the first item and ask your question

Move to the second item and ask your question again.

Continue in this way until you have checked all the items you are trying to choose between. It is better if you try to narrow it down using your instinct and normal decision making methods before you start to dowse. You really don't want to dowse over every pair of shoes in the shop!

As with all dowsing, the larger and smoother the indicator action, the stronger the answer. If your 'yes' indicator is a clockwise circle, the larger and smoother the circle the stronger the 'yes'.

If your indicator movement is small or ragged, you could be asking the wrong question. Try and rethink your question and be more specific.

If you're still not getting a clear answer, it might well be that there isn't a clear answer. One item is as good as the next.

If that happens and you can't really tell why, you can dowse to try and clarify the problem

do you need either item at all?

do you really need both? Try to stay neutral!

are they equally good / useful to you?

Often your question will not be about an actual object but an idea or a decision that you have to make.

You could be trying to make a choice between two holiday destinations or different types of holiday. Write each different choice on a slip of paper or print out the holiday details or use the individual page from the brochure and work with the dowsing pendulum over each one.

As always, it's important to clarify your question. The round the world cruise might be perfect for you, but that doesn't help if you don't have the time or the money to be able to take it in your next summer holiday.

If you are dowsing about a holiday, you need to focus on when this holiday is to be taken and who you are going on holiday with. The dowsing pendulum may give you a clear indication that a luxury spa is definitely the right choice. But that won't help if you are thinking about a girl's weekend away and you really need to choose a family holiday.

You may be deciding about a new car, and this might need a series of questions such as what style of car, should you buy new or used, should you buy diesel or petrol. Once you've narrowed the choice down, you may be left with a decision between different makes in a certain size of car, and eventually you may be trying to choose between two specific vehicles.

For most of this process, you wouldn't take your dowsing pendulum to the actual cars. Simply write the make or model or size or engine type on pieces of paper. As you work through the decision-making process, keep writing out new slips of paper for each stage of dowsing.

At each stage place the pieces of paper on a clear table in front of you - don't allow clutter to get in the way.

Once you have narrowed it down to a choice between two or more actual vehicles, you could either write their descriptions or registration numbers onto slips of paper and continue as before, or you could visit the actual vehicles with your dowsing pendulum.

The same is true of any decision you have to make. When you are working with your dowsing pendulum you must think the process through before you start, to ensure that you have the right questions.

Career decisions.

The decisions we make about our careers create the framework for our entire lives and far too often they're not really decisions at all. In matters where we should be taking real care over each decision, we don't even think them through at all, we just drift.

So many people are in jobs that they hate, trapped in the 9 to 5 and just living for the end of the working day, the end of the working week, and in many cases the end of the working life. You shouldn't have to spend a lifetime just looking forward to retirement.

Far too many people take a career path that somebody else has chosen for them. Parents, teachers or career officers, or sometimes just blind luck, taking you into the first job that was offered.

But we spend so much of our lives in work that we really should invest a little bit of time in trying to decide what we actually want to do. After all, you're far more likely to be successful if you are doing something you actually like doing.

At the end of the day, although money is very important, it certainly isn't everything. You can be very rich, and still miserable. Although everybody needs a certain amount of money to be able to pay the bills, once that is taken care of, you also need to be able to enjoy life. There's not much point in having a big house, the big car or even the big yacht, if you don't have any time to be able to enjoy them.

You may have a choice of two career opportunities which could be a simple 'one or the other' choice. But one may involve moving, or taking a cut in income for a long term gain. Some decisions are complex and may require a series of questions to sort out the answers to each stage.

- Would I be happy in another part of the country?
- Do I want security now?
- Do I want a long term opportunity?
- Do I want position A?
- Do I want position B?

Again, the list is almost endless – you can use your dowsing pendulum in any situation where you are having a problem making a decision.

Try not to become totally dependent on your pendulum – there's really no need to check if you should get up in the morning! But there are plenty of decisions where it can be extremely helpful, especially when you feel a tug between instinct and logic.

Some decisions can involve a lot of money – buying a car, building an extension or fitting double glazing, making an investment, buying a pension. In this type of case you want to ensure that you are making the right decision because it's not easy to fix any mistake you might make.

Other decisions might affect you for a long time, choosing a university, choosing what to study, deciding to change career or leave a secure job, choosing a school for your child.

Then there are decisions that cost you your time. Do you choose event A or B? A walking holiday or a week on the beach? Learning Cordon Bleu cookery or watercolour painting?

Working through endless decisions is all part of life and actually making the decisions instead of allowing someone else to make them for you, can make life so much richer. You can take control rather than drifting

The whole process of working with your dowsing pendulum can help you regain that control, not only the actual dowsing, but the preparation. The actual process of thinking about what your choices and questions are means that you are taking control and dowsing - done properly and seriously - will lead you to the correct choices for you at that time.

9

Dowsing the elements.

When we first think of dowsing, we automatically think of water divining, the craft of using rods to find a source of water hidden underground. This is a technique that has been used throughout human history. After all, water is a vital element for life, and when it is not visibly flowing on the surface it can be difficult to pinpoint.

As a child on the west coast of Ireland, my mother was the one they would send out when looking for a source of water in a field and it's technique that is equally valid today and works just as well with the dowsing pendulum as with dowsing rods.

It can certainly be very useful if you know that there is a water leak in the pipes underground, but you're not quite sure where in the pipework the actual break is.

You can of course dowse for other minerals in the ground, such as gold and silver, gas and oil or gemstones. When the American dowser Verne Cameron, was invited to go to South Africa, it was to help pinpoint their mineral wealth, and the government of the United States of America took his ability so seriously that the CIA decided he was a security risk, and they refused to issue him with a passport.

Although you may not find yourself panning for gold or searching for a sapphire mine, you can certainly use the dowsing pendulum to help you choose your healing crystals, either choosing them in the first place, or deciding which ones you need to use for a particular problem.

As with all dowsing, you need to be very clear in your question when using a pendulum, to help you with choosing a healing crystal. There is a big difference between the questions;

- Is amethyst, a good energy for me?
- Is this amethyst, a good energy for me?
- Is this amethyst, a good energy to help me avoid headaches when using a computer?
- is this amethyst, a good energy for treating this client's problem (state problem)?

Clarity in the question is vital in all dowsing.

Archaeological dowsing is a very active area of dowsing and this can certainly be an area where you are dosing the elements, trying to find what is hidden in the ground, often just as traces of organic matter left in the soil.

Archaeological dowsing can involve both dowsing on actual sites and map dowsing, where you dowse over a map to pinpoint areas of interest. The British Society of Dowsers has a great deal of information about this area of dowsing and they run regular field trips and events and if you're interested in history, it's certainly an area where you can bring together your love of history, dowsing and getting together with other like-minded people.

Dowsing earth energies.

Of course not all energies can be seen. We all accept this quite happily in areas that can be easily proven. We know that electricity is invisible most of the time, but we also know that it's there, that it works, when we plug something in it turns on. Everybody will also accept magnetism. After all, you put a fridge magnet on the fridge and stays there.

But not everybody accepts that different types of magnetism and electromagnetic fields can affect our health. And imagine what an electric light would have seemed like to somebody 500 years ago. It could have got you burned as a witch!

The earth is full of energy fields which were accepted by our ancestors. They built many of the great monuments to coincide with these energies, whether that was in areas of sacred geometry, or on the Ley Lines or Dragon Lines that are believed to carry a form of the Earth's magnetic field in straight lines across the planet.

Working with dowsing is a wonderful way of being able to pick up these invisible energies, whatever your interest in them. You may have a deep interest in the ancient energies of standing stones and stone circles. You may want to work with the Dragon lines in your feng shui practice. You may want to protect your own health and that of your family from Geopathic and electromagnetic stress.

Before you can do any work with these energy fields. You have to know where they are and whether they are having a positive or negative effect on you. This is where working with your dowsing pendulum comes in.

- Calm your thoughts and empty your mind of negative energies. Try to distance yourself from any emotions you might feel about the area.
- Take a deep breath and let it out slowly.
- Hold the pendulum between the thumb and forefinger, letting your wrist relax.
- Ask the pendulum to show you whether the energy is negative or positive
- the pendulum will hold its neutral position until it finds an energy source and as always, the larger the movement of the pendulum the stronger the energy.

An area of strong positive energy can be wonderfully recharging to your whole energy system, making you feel better, lighter, giving you a more positive outlook on life and improving health problems. When you find one of these areas try to make it a regular part of your schedule to spend time there to recharge your energy system.

At the other end of the scale an area of negative energy can be very detrimental to your well-being and if at all possible you should try and avoid it. If you can't avoid it try and introduce feng shui cures to minimise the effect or protect your personal energy field by wearing healing crystals such as obsidian, black tourmaline or amethyst.

I have done many fairs and events over the years, many of which have been in ancient castles that have collected a variety of energies to themselves over the centuries and some are more comfortable to work in than others.

One example was a country fair in the fields below a castle which has been the centre of power and power struggles for almost a thousand years.

There were a number of large marquees pitched on the field and a craft fair was in one of these on the edge of the event. Although we had done this event in previous years, and thoroughly enjoyed the atmosphere, there was something wrong this time, and a group of us were all suffering from headaches, tiredness, and to be honest, irritability! When I dowsed that area of the marquee, I found that we were at a point of very negative energy that went specifically through that part of the marquee. Unfortunately we couldn't move the tent or our stalls, So all I could do for the rest of that weekend was trying to reduce the effect as much as possible by placing natural points of clear quartz crystal around the area to deflect the energy away from where people were.

The area of earth energies is a huge subject worthy of a number of books all to itself, so I can only begin to scratch the surface here. If you are interested in learning more, there are many books and websites for you to explore with many different approaches to the subject. Just look around until you find one you are comfortable with.

10

Dowsing for good health

This can be one of the most personally important areas in which you can use a dowsing pendulum.

In our modern world, we have lost contact with nature. Many people don't understand where their food comes from - apart from the fact that it comes from the nearest supermarket. We have lost the connection between us and the soil and nature, and it's no wonder that so many of us suffer from illnesses and general poor health that can be traced back to food choices or more specifically, lack of choice and poor choices.

Dowsing is also a very useful way of checking that any vitamins or food supplements are the right ones for you to use.

We have also become too reliant on medication. Assuming that it can solve every problem, rather than being willing to take some control for our health ourselves.

You are what you eat

It is often said that we are what we eat - and that is very true – but although we repeat it glibly, very few of us actually think about what it means and understand exactly what food does what!

So how many of us really know if we are eating what is best for us?

Not many!

Using the dowsing pendulum means that it is easy to check that we are indeed eating the best type of food for our health.

You can start with a simple list of the types of food you normally eat.

Simply dowse over the food that you are checking. Either line up your selection of actual foods or write their names on separate pieces of paper. You can do with for general food groups or specific brands or varieties, for instance a choice of toast, cereal or boiled egg for breakfast, or a choice of different types or brands of cereal.

Keep each food or slip of paper separate as you are working. Dowse over each one individually in turn, asking the pendulum if that food is good for you at this particular time. You can do this over different types of food, or even over different ways of preparing the same food.

Once you do start thinking about food, and the fact that we are what we eat, you will begin to realise how important food choices are to health and general wellbeing and you will want to take more care and give more thought to those choices.

But it can be difficult to work out what foods are good for you personally, or what could be causing some health problems. So unsurprisingly, a large industry has grown up around this uncertainty, taking advantage of our confusion and testing us for allergies and food intolerances, very often causing even more confusion and distress.

These types of problem with different foods and the way we react to them are very good areas in which to work with your dowsing pendulum.

If you are worried about food allergies and intolerances, ask your pendulum.

If you do actually have an allergy or intolerance for that specific food group, such as wheat or dairy, you can also narrow it down. For instance, I don't have a wheat intolerance, but I do have a problem with a preservative that they add to a lot of processed breads - it gives me hiccups! So if I'm thinking of trying a new or different bread supply, I can dowse first of all asking the question:-

Will this particular type/brand of bread give me hiccups?

It can also be even more specific - will this loaf, give me hiccups?

Either of those questions are very specific and should give me a very clear answer. However, if I asked the question 'will bread give me hiccups?', the dowsing pendulum wouldn't be able to give me a question, because some breads do cause the problem and other breads don't.

Whether you choose to do your pendulum dowsing actually in the shop or not is entirely up to you! I have to admit, that although it may not raise eyebrows at all in your local organic farm shop, you might get some very strange looks in your local big supermarket and your family may choose not to be with you in future!

As well as asking about the effect of specific food groups on your system, you can also check foods for their general health properties. Many fruits are sprayed with chemicals, which you might prefer to avoid, while others are irradiated to keep them fresh.

As any area of pendulum dowsing, the idea is to help you make decisions, rather than to ask the pendulum about every decision. Work with your pendulum to discover the foods that are good for your health, and the foods that are definitely not good for your health, and then use this information to make your own decisions in daily life. You only need to refer back to your pendulum if you are considering new choices, or some problems have developed.

You must also take care that you do not overreact and end up restricting your diet to a dangerous degree. We are bombarded with warnings about food, and the dangers to our health of too much coffee, not enough/too much red wine, too much fruit causing acid problems, or too many takeaways - all of which will kill us according to the media. Sometimes it seems as if every week brings some new danger in our food. If you listened to all the scare stories you'd begin to believe that the safest thing would be to starve yourself!

But the fact of the matter is, even if it doesn't make great headlines, we are designed to be able to process most foods in moderation, and the aim is to work out what is a healthy balanced diet for us, allowing some treats along the way.

Vitamins, Minerals and herbal supplements

Foods are not the only thing that we choose blindly without really understanding what we're swallowing. We often take a myriad of different vitamins, minerals and supplements, often without really understanding why. We assume that if the tablets come from a health food shop they are bound to be good for us. But that might not always be the case. I've often heard the words, but it's natural, it must be all right. Don't forget, Deadly Nightshade is natural, but its name gives you a bit of a clue about it!

Some supplements interact badly with some prescribed medication. It is possible to overdose on certain vitamins, and whilst some herbal medicines may be a very important addition to our diet others might have no affect on us at all, and simply cost us money. So although I am a fan of vitamins and supplements and some herbal remedies, I do like to make sure that they are a positive addition to my regime, rather than causing a problem themselves.

So this is another area where your dowsing pendulum can help you sort out what you should and should not be taking.

If you already have a specific tablet or herbal medicine, you can dowse directly over the bottle, asking your question. Again, there are differences between:

- Is all right for me to take this vitamin?
- Is this vitamin doing me positive good?

After all, it might be perfectly all right for you to be taking a vitamin, not causing you any harm, but not doing any good either in which case it's harming your wallet.

If you are worried about deficiencies in your diet, you can also use your pendulum to check if you do actually suffer from a deficiency. Again, phrase your question clearly. You will not necessarily get the same answer from the two questions:-

- Can I take a supplement of vitamin C?
- Do I need to take a supplement of vitamin C?

You can also use your dowsing pendulum to check a combination of supplements. Tablet A and tablet B might be fine if you take them on their own, but they might not be very good if you take them together and many people regularly take a combination of five or six or even more different vitamins, supplements and herbal remedies.

Although there is nothing wrong with this on its own, and there may be very good reasons to take all of them, it can be worthwhile asking your dowsing pendulum if the combination of these specific supplements is good for you.

If you receive a negative, you can then either remove one supplement at a time and ask the question again until you find the culprit or a quicker method is to ask if you would be better leaving one of the supplements out of your mix. You can do this by dowsing over each individual supplement. Again you can either do this with the actual tablets or by writing their exact names on the separate pieces of paper and dowsing over the papers.

If you are worried about a prescription medication, you can use your dowsing pendulum for this question as well. But you should never, under any circumstances, stop taking a prescription medication without consulting your medical practitioner.

Use a series of questions to try and pinpoint exactly what your problem is with the medication, and then go and discuss your concerns with your doctor.

Balancing energy with a dowsing pendulum.

So far, we have worked with the dowsing pendulum to give a 'positive/negative', 'yes/no' answer to a question. But there is another method of working with a pendulum, balancing energy.

This is where you allow the pendulum to energise something by infusing positive energy or by removing the negative energies from an area or item.

In this case, you let the pendulum know what you want it to do and then allow it to move until it comes to a halt on its own. As always, just hold it lightly between your thumb and forefinger.

For instance, if your feet are hurting from a long day standing, you can ask your pendulum to unwind the pain, holding it over your foot and allowing it to swing until it comes to a halt once it has unwound the pain or removed negative energy.

The pattern it makes, whether clockwise/anti clockwise or backwards and forwards doesn't matter and you don't need to try and influence it.

If the pain or problem is temporary, for instance, too many hours on your feet, the pendulum may swing wildly at first (your feet are very sore) but come to a halt quite quickly.

If you are dealing with a more deep-seated or long-term problem, the pendulum will probably take much longer to come to rest.

If you are dealing with a serious long-term problem you should be careful about simply removing the pain, because in some cases, the pain is a warning sign and you shouldn't just keep getting rid of it, whether by pendulum dowsing or taking painkillers.

You should try and find the source of the pain and again, you can work with your dowsing pendulum to try and narrow the possibilities, but you should also go to your doctor or, if you're working on someone else, advise them to consult their doctor.

You can also use this form of pendulum dowsing to scan the body to find a problem area. Many French physicians and chiropractors work with the dowsing pendulum to pinpoint problems in the spine or other areas of the body.

If you are going to work with your pendulum in this area, you need to be aware that you could be dealing with quite a lot of negative energy. So it is even more important than normal to make sure that you're calm, surround yourself with positive energy and keep your intentions or question very clear.

Calm your mind, sit or stand comfortably, take a deep breath and focus.

Ask your pendulum to help you find the source of the specific problem.

If you are working on someone else, slowly move your hand and the dowsing pendulum across their body. It is always best to work along the line of the spine, using the chakra system from the root chakra at the base of the spine, up to the Crown chakra above the head. (see next chapter for more information about the Chakra system).

The pendulum will hold its neutral position until it finds an area of negative energy and at that point, it will begin to move. Allow it to come to a halt on its own to try and bring some relief and make a note of the area of the body where the pendulum is reacting.

If it does react, wait until it has come to its neutral position and then move slowly on up the line of the spine to see if there are any further points of negative energy.

If you are working on your own energy system, hold your dowsing pendulum in front of you, and imagine that you are travelling through your chakra system, focusing on each part of your spine clearly mentally, resting at each chakra and allowing your pendulum to react.

There is much more information on the chakra system and how to work with your dowsing pendulum on the system in the next chapter.

You can also use this method of dowsing to energise water or food with positive energy.

Again, clear your mind and focus, surround yourself in a bubble of positive energy.

Focus clearly on the item and ask your pendulum to infuse it with positive energy.

Allow the pendulum to move until it comes to a halt on its own. This process will become more natural and easier to do the more often you do it.

You can use a similar process for distant healing. This is when you want to send healing energy to someone when you cannot visit them in person, and it can be used over hundreds or even thousands of miles.

You must always ask the permission of the person before you do any healing work. Show respect and do not try to force healing on someone who does not want it or is not ready to accept it.

Once you have their permission focus your mind very clearly on that person and on the purpose of your healing energy. It isn't any good being very general, with some comment such as 'help this person to feel better'. You need to focus your attention on the specific problem, whether it is physical or emotional, mental or spiritual.

Once you have clearly set your healing intention in your mind and balanced your own energy, allow the pendulum to move until it comes to rest on its own.

As you become more comfortable with your dowsing pendulum you will find areas that you are drawn to personally and you will develop your own ways of working with your pendulum to improve your own health, and that of those around you.

11

The Chakra System

The dowsing pendulum is a very helpful tool for working on and balancing the Chakra system, but what is the Chakra system?

Ancient Indian Sanskrit texts teach us of the Chakra system. They tell of centres of energy in the human body, with seven major points arranged along the line of the spine.

During our daily life, they can become unbalanced, which can hinder the flow of energy throughout the body. Over time this can contribute to illness or emotional upset.

We are very complex systems, and many illnesses cannot be treated simply. All parts of our body interact with others and we should treat ourselves as a whole rather than as a collection of parts.

The effects can be physical, mental, emotional or spiritual and, because we are 'whole' beings rather than a machine made up of spare parts, emotional stress can cause physical illness, mental pressure can cause problems spiritually.

We understand that something like depression can lead to chronic ill health. Understanding the inter-related nature of our energy fields and chakras is just a few further steps. Keeping our energy system in balance is a vital part of maintaining our general well-being.

In Eastern Yogic texts, the chakras are visualised as lotus flowers, with the petals and fine roots of the flower distributing the life force – or Prana – throughout the physical body and converting the energy into chemical, hormonal and cellular changes.

The seven major chakras

The Root Chakra (1st)

Located at the base of the spine.

This is the chakra that controls our ability to be grounded. It is associated with physical energy and physical health. If this is blocked you can feel anxious, insecure, frustrated. Physically it can cover osteoarthritis, obesity, problems with the feet and legs, haemorrhoids and constipation and chronic long term illnesses.

Colours: Red, black, dark brown

Crystals: red Jasper, red tiger's eye, ruby, garnet, hematite, pietersite, smoky quartz, black tourmaline, black onyx

The Sacral Chakra (2nd)

Located 1" below the navel.

This balances sexuality, emotion, desire, creativity, intuition and self worth. If it is blocked you may feel emotionally explosive, lacking energy, have feelings of isolation. Physically it can lead to kidney and uterine disorders, lower back pain, impotence and prostate problems

Colour: orange

Crystals: carnelian, orange calcite, aragonite, amber, orange sapphire

The Solar Plexus Chakra (3rd)

Located below the breastbone and behind the stomach.

From the back of the body, it is just below the shoulder blades. It is also known as the power chakra and is associated with personal power, ambition, anger and joy, intellectual activity and the central nervous system. If this chakra is blocked you can lack confidence, worry about the opinions of others, be oversensitive to criticism, suffer low self esteem or have an addictive personality. Physically it can cover digestive problems, stomach ulcers, diabetes, chronic fatigue and allergies.

Colour: yellow

Crystals: citrine, yellow sapphire, golden tiger's eye, yellow jasper

The Heart Chakra (4th)

Located in the centre of the chest at the heart area.

It is associated with compassion, love and spirituality. When this chakra is out of balance you feel indecisive, paranoid, fear betrayal or generally feel sorry for yourself. Physically it can lead to heart disease, asthma, high blood pressure, lung disease and cancers. It can also cover problems with the arms, hands and fingers.

Colour: Green, pink

Crystals: aventurine, malachite, jade, peridot, emerald, rose quartz, kunzite, morganite, rhodochrosite, unakite

The Throat Chakra (5th)

Located just below the collar bone in the throat area of the neck.

It is associated with self-expression, communication, voice and the expression of creativity through speech and writing. If it is out of balance you can feel that you want to hold back, an inability to express emotions, blocked creativity or perfectionism. Physically it can cover colds, sore throats, hearing and thyroid problems and tinnitus.

Colour: blue

Crystals: lapis lazuli, sodalite, aquamarine, blue lace agate, sapphire, turquoise, chrysocolla

The Third Eye Chakra (6th)

Located between and just above the eyes.

It is associated with intuition, psychic ability, energies of the spirit and the elimination of selfish attitudes. If it is out of balance you may feel afraid of success, non-assertive or the opposite, egotistical. Physically it can lead to headaches, nightmares, eye problems and poor vision or neurological disturbances.

Colour: indigo

Crystals: amethyst, sugilite, charoite, fluorite, lepidolite, iolite

The Crown Chakra (7th)

Located at the crown, just beyond the top of the skull.

This chakra is associated with enlightenment, spirituality, energy and wisdom. If this chakra is blocked there may be a constant sense of frustration, confusion, depression, obsession, no spark of joy. Physically it can cover a sensitivity to pollutants, epilepsy or chronic exhaustion.

Colour: clear, violet

Crystals: clear quartz, diamond, selenite, danburite, amethyst, tanzanite

Other minor chakras

Minor chakras – where fewer energy flows intersect - are found in other areas of the body. For instance, the palm of the hand, the sole of the foot, in front of the ear and behind the eye, above each breast and at the back of the knee.

Dowsing to rebalancing the Chakra system

The pendulum can be used to re-balance the chakra system and to pinpoint problem areas by dowsing over each of the chakras in turn.

Obviously you can't use this method on yourself.

Ask the person whose chakras you will be cleansing, to lie down comfortably. If this is not possible, you can use the method while they are sitting comfortably with their hands by their sides.

Ask the pendulum to help you in balancing the chakras. You may be trying to ease a specific problem, such as back ache or a headache, ask the pendulum to help you in this aim.

Start at the root chakra and allow the pendulum to move as it wishes. If it stays in your neutral position, the chakra is balanced. If it moves in either your positive or negative pattern, allow the pendulum to move as it wishes, holding it over the chakra until it settles once more into the neutral position, showing that the chakra has been rebalanced, then move onto the next chakra.

Continue this until you have passed over all the chakras, ending at the crown.

Once the chakras have been balanced, especially if there has been a strong blockage in one of the upper chakras, the person may feel lightheaded or slightly dizzy. This is quite normal, he or she should sit quietly for a minute or two, try to have a drink of water available.

Cleanse the pendulum between working on cleansing chakra systems, you don't want to transfer negative energy between people or healing sessions.

There are many ways of cleansing a pendulum. If you choose a crystal pendulum - as I prefer - you can use the same method you would choose for any other crystal.

The methods I prefer are to either lay the pendulum on a bed of amethyst for three or four hours, or to place the pendulum in a small, clear glass bowl and sit this bowl in a larger clear glass bowl filled with dry sea salt, again for three or four hours. You can also cleanse your pendulum by clearing your mind and imagining a stream of pure while light washing over the pendulum.

Dowsing to Cleanse your own chakras

You can also use your pendulum to cleanse your own chakras - although obviously not by dowsing directly over them.

Clear your mind and sit or stand somewhere comfortable.

Ask the pendulum to help you in balancing your chakras.

Whichever hand you dowse with, hold the other palm over, but not touching your root chakra and hold the pendulum away to the side of your body.

As with cleansing chakras on someone else, the pendulum will either remain neutral, indicating that the chakra is in balance, or it will move. If it does start to move, allow it to move as it wishes, for as long as it wishes. Once it comes back to your neutral position you can move your palm over the next chakra.

Alternatively you can focus mentally on each Chakra as you balance it rather than holding your hand over the area.

You can use this method on a single chakra to help ease a specific pain - for instance on your throat chakra if you have a sore throat or a cold, on your sacral chakra if you have indigestion or a stomach upset, or on your third eye if you have a headache.

However, you should not get into the habit of overworking one area as this will cause imbalance in the system as a whole.

12

Dowsing and the home.

We are often unknowingly surrounded by negative energy in our home or at work, and this can be very detrimental to our health on all levels, emotional and mental, spiritual and physical. Very often, we can simply feel unwell or unhappy, without really knowing what the cause is.

Working with the dowsing pendulum can help clarify where problems may lie, helping you work out how to solve them or avoid them in the first place.

Choosing a new home

There are many ways in which you can work with your dowsing pendulum while you are looking for a new home and it can help avoid all the heartache, pain and expense of choosing the wrong one.

Your home and the energy in it is vitally important to your general health and well-being on all levels. It should be your sanctuary, your escape, your place of security and comfort. But none of this will be the case if the energy of your home is incompatible with your personal energy.

When you're in the first stages of looking for a new home - whether buying or renting - work with your dowsing pendulum to help you choose the right area in which to look for a property. You can do this by dowsing over a map either of the local area or region or country.

In fact, if you are looking for a property abroad, you can dowse over a map of the larger area to begin with, to help you narrow down the country you want to look at. For instance, you may be trying to decide between France and Spain, or between a holiday home in Italy or Scotland. You may have decided that you want a second home in America, but not have made your decision about which State to choose. You may want to relocate entirely but can't decide between Australia and Canada.

When you are dowsing over a map, spread the map on a clear table. Don't put anything else on the table, as you don't want the pendulum to be distracted by another item. For instance, a favourite ornament that you brought back from a holiday in one country might influence the pendulum dowsing.

Calm your mind and think clearly about your question. Try not to let emotion influence you. For instance, your choice of a holiday home will also have

79

to allow for the ease of getting to it, how often you're likely to be able to use it, whether you are able to earn income by letting it out if this is important to you, whether it's a good investment. Sometimes, what we think is perfect, and what we really want, will in truth, lead to a lot of trouble and stress because it simply isn't practical. Working with your pendulum should lead you through this minefield, so that you can find the right answer for you.

The same sort of process is true when you are choosing your home rather than a holiday home.

The area you think you want, might not actually be the area that is right for you. The whole idea of working with your dowsing pendulum is to allow you to find the right answer, rather than to confirm the answer you want.

Once you have narrowed the area, you can also dowse over the details of different properties to check them before you visit.

Take the advert or the estate agents information or just the address written on a piece of paper.

Clear your mind of any emotional attachment to the property. At this stage, you must forget that there are pretty roses round the door, that it's in the area you've always wanted, that it's very close to a school. You are asking if this particular house or flat has the right energy for you and your family.

This type of question is a very good example of how specific you must be in how you phrase your question.

For instance, you could ask simply, is this the right home for me and my family? Do you have a specific timescale in mind? It might not be the right long-term home, but it might be exactly the right home for the next two years. So the question should really be. Is this the right home for me and my family at the moment? Asking the first question might mean that you miss out on something that is perfect for you in the short term.

Once you have cleared your mind and focused on your question, hold your pendulum over the address or details and allow it to give you your answer.

You can also ask other more specific questions. Questions about

- the structure of the building,
- the energy of the property
- the correct price,
- how long it might take to complete a sale.

Think carefully about what you might want to know about a new home and then form your questions. Choosing a new home is one of the biggest, most important and most expensive decisions you will make. It's worth spending some time on getting that decision right.

You can also take your dowsing pendulum with you when you are viewing houses or flats.

In this case, you might be actually checking the energy in the building, asking your pendulum to show you whether the energy is negative or positive. You already know all the movements that your pendulum uses to show you negative and positive, so if your 'yes' answer is a clockwise circle and that is the movement that your pendulum makes, then it's picking up positive energy. As always, the larger circle the stronger the energy.

We've probably all entered a building and felt either comfortable or uncomfortable. Dowsing helps us to clarify that feeling before making a very costly mistake.

You can also dowse more physical attributes. Is the building sound? Is an area of damp important or just a minor problem? Does the new decorating in one room hide something that will give you trouble in the future? Obviously you still need a surveyors report, but this can help clarify some of your questions.

Dowsing your existing home

There are times when reorganising the use of rooms or the placement of furniture can make your home more comfortable and your dowsing pendulum can help you work out the right areas of energy for each purpose.

Sometimes, you may feel the room doesn't feel quite right or that there are some areas of your life that are not working as you would wish. If you work with feng shui principles, you can incorporate your dowsing pendulum when you are working on the correct layout for your home.

The first stage in this process is to dowse your home room by room, checking the energy in each room. At this stage you are asking the pendulum to show you whether the energy is positive or negative. Once you have created the energy map of your home you can begin to work on any areas that have shown negative energy. You could introduce feng shui cures such as hanging crystals to move stale Chi, or you could work with healing crystals to counter any negative energies you have found.

You may find that you need to change the use of some rooms. A room you may be using as an office could be better as a bedroom and the existing bedroom changed into an office. You can either dowse in the actual spot or over a sketch of the house plan or room plan. This process can be a little like the old childhood game of hotter and colder.

You start with quite a general question. Would this room make good office for me? If you get a 'no', you can move on through either different rooms or different purposes for that room. Once you get a 'yes', you can move on to more specific questions about the placement of pieces of furniture or equipment.

You can ask the help of your dowsing pendulum in all sorts of decision-making.

For instance, if you are redecorating it is vitally important to choose colours that will suit you and your family and your lifestyle. Colours can have a huge impact on your health and well-being, and it's far more efficient if you can make these decisions before you stand back and look at the newly decorated room and realise you've made a mistake.

You can also work with your dowsing pendulum when you are choosing new furniture or carpets. Again, getting this wrong can be a costly and time-consuming mistake.

Choosing the position for pictures or ornaments is much easier to rectify, but there are times when you just can't get it right. No matter how many different ways you hang the pictures they still don't look right!

And on the subject of hanging pictures, you can work with your dowsing pendulum to check that you are not about to bash a nail right through something vitally important!

There are also times when there is a problem in the house that you just can't pinpoint. For instance, if you have a number of pieces of electrical equipment that are all connected, when something goes wrong with the system as a whole it can be very time consuming to track down where the actual fault is. It could be one of the pieces of equipment, or it could be one of the connecting cables - there are times when even the experts work on the system of trial and error, keep changing different things until you find what works, especially if it's an intermittent problem. It can save a lot of time and frustration if you spend a little bit of time with your dowsing pendulum at the beginning of the problem.

Although not strictly in the home, your car is certainly part of the home and you can work with the same dowsing pendulum system to track down faults in a vehicle, especially those irritating and difficult intermittent electrical faults.

As you get more used to working with your dowsing pendulum and more comfortable with it, you will find areas of life and areas of your home where it becomes an indispensable tool for you.

Getting work done on your home can be fraught with difficulties. The last thing you want is a rogue tradesmen in your home and in your life.

When you are looking for suppliers, builders or other professionals, you can use your pendulum to dowse through the phone book, check cards or leaflets that have come through the door or even the details of someone recommended to you.

You will probably use a series of questions for this dowsing, for instance

- Is this person/company trustworthy?
- Is this person/company reliable?
- Does this person/company give fair quotations

But even once you've established that the tradesman is a reliable and trustworthy person, there are still other questions that you need to take into account. Each project will be different and personal to you and your family, which means that each set of questions will also be different. Think about the project in mind and think about what your questions should be. Some examples are:-

- Is this the right person/company for this project?
- Will I be comfortable working with this person/company in my home?
- How long will the projects take?
- Will the project run over budget?

You can use this same approach for various other types of supplier for your home, especially when an expensive purchase is involved or long-term working relationship is in question, such as finding a new gardener or a cleaning service.

13

Dowsing and the Garden

All of us like plants in our home and in our garden if we are lucky enough to have one. And of course, we like them to be happy and healthy.

Your dowsing pendulum can be a very successful tool when you are working with plants. It can help you decide which plants to place where in the garden. Plants can be very particular about position. Is the soil right? Is the light right? Is the moisture right?

A few years ago I had a shrub that wouldn't settle in at all. It was dug up and replanted in four different parts of the garden, all of which should have been all right for it but weren't. It survived, but it certainly didn't thrive until I took my dowsing pendulum and went around the garden, asking the pendulum to show me where this particular shrub would be happy. Eventually it gave a very strong, positive answer, and the shrub was duly re-homed again. This time it thrived and now has to be pruned almost every year.

You can work with your dowsing pendulum to choose plants in the first place, either from the catalogue or at the garden centre and then to choose where you should plant them once you get them home.

The right soil and healthy soil is a basic building block for any successful garden, so work with your dowsing pendulum to find out what type of soil you have to work with (chalky or acid) and which nutrients you should add to your soil to make it healthy for your plants.

There are a number of stages in the process where you can ask the help of your pendulum in ensuring that you are making the right decision – which can save your plants a lot of grief and you a lot of money.

Plants react very well to dowsing. After all, they are very much part of the natural environment and the pendulum can pick up whether they are happy or not in their surroundings. Whether they are healthy and have been grown naturally rather than forced. The life force is much stronger in a plant that has had the right time to mature naturally.

Planning a garden

At the very first stages of planning your garden, you will of course do the basics.

Check which way it faces – north or south, do you get the sun in the morning or the evening or all the way through the day.

Check the soil – is it acid or chalky? Lime or clay?

Decide what you want to do with your garden – grow vegetables, have a rose garden, a garden for children or a garden for drinking a nice glass of wine.

You can work with your dowsing pendulum to help you make the decisions about how you want to use your garden. Just use the decision making techniques with your dowsing pendulum.

Write the ideas on separate pieces of paper and dowse over them. You might find that you are getting the 'yes' indicator for more than one plan. A place for the children to play and a barbeque area for the adults as well as a spot for quiet sunbathing. Very few gardens will have only one use, but you can use your pendulum to help you decide which are the most important areas for you, and therefore how much of the overall space you should allocate for each use.

Once you have your plans sorted you get to the exciting part – choosing plants!

If you are really organised and you are going to set out a garden plan with planting lists and designs, you can dowse to find out which plant families and then which specimens you should choose.

Again, you can write the possible ideas on pieces of paper and dowse over them. You'll have done some research before you get to this stage, so you don't have to go through the entire plant encyclopaedia, but once you've narrowed your ideas down, the pendulum can help you focus your ideas into a manageable list before you decide to start visiting the garden centres and nurseries.

Picking and planting

Once you actually get to the garden centre, your pendulum can begin to help you in more specific ways with questions about an actual plant before you decide to spend your money on it.

Will the plant thrive in the conditions you can offer it?

Is it suitable for the type of gardening you can offer it – is it a high maintenance diva when you want a low maintenance garden?

Which part of your garden design should you plant it in? Imagine the area of the garden clearly as you ask if it is right or not.

Is the actual plant healthy?

How many of that type of plant should you buy. One, three, five? Apparently they look better in odd numbers!

Do you need some special treatment for the plant. Special compost? Plant food? Plant supports?

When you have chosen the plants, filled your car and carried them all into the garden, your pendulum can still be helpful.

You can dowse to check where in the garden you should plant it. It might like some shade, or prefer the sun, or just really not like that tree you were going to put it beside. Plants can be as temperamental as any other living thing – but find the right spot and they'll reward you for years.

You can use three methods to find the right position before you actually start digging holes.

You can position yourself in the middle of your garden and slowly turn in a circle as you dowse – asking the pendulum to show you the right direction. Then you can go to the section of your garden that it indicated.

If you have a drawing of your garden plan, you can dowse over that, asking the pendulum to indicate with a positive when you are over the best area.

You can go the actual part of the garden you have in mind and dowse in that particular area, to check that you have chosen the right area, and to fine tune your selection – front or back of the border?

Once your plants are happily settled into their new home, you can still continue to work with your pendulum to keep them happy and healthy. You can check what kind of care you should give a plant. When to feed, when to prune, whether it's time to split a group of plants.

If things do start to go wrong, you can use your pendulum to try and find out why.

- Is the soil right?
- Does it need fertilizer or a feed?
- Is it being watered too little or too much?
- Does it need pruning?

- Would it like to be moved?

Houseplants

You can also ask your pendulum for guidance if you are choosing a plant for the house.

Have you placed it in the right position in your home?

- Does it need more or less sunlight?
- Are you under or over watering?
- Does the plant need feeding?
- Does it need re-potting?

Vegetable Gardening

Dowsing can be particularly helpful when you are growing plants for food or good health. We are all becoming more interested in our food. Is it grown organically or is it full of pesticides? How many food miles has it travelled? Is it really fresh? Does it have any flavour?

More and more of us are setting aside some part of a garden as a vegetable plot, or growing in pots on the patio, or even a balcony and of course, allotments are becoming very popular again.

When you are growing vegetables, fruit or herbs for healthy eating or as herbal medicine, you can work with your pendulum throughout the entire process.

First of all you can check that you are planning to grow the right plants. There's such a huge range of food that you can grow and it can be a bit overwhelming, so dowsing can really help you focus your thoughts.

What are you growing them for – a large chunk of your main food supply or special treats?

Are you growing special vegetables that are hard to get in the shops?

Do you cook food for a growing family or are you a gourmet, loving to experiment with new ingredients?

Is organic produce important to you – it's more work than using chemicals but many people wouldn't grow their food any other way

Have you got time to dedicate to a demanding crop or do you want plants that just get on with growing?

How much space do you have or do you want to use for your vegetable garden?

Are you more interested in healing herbs or food for the pot

Once you have your ideas clear, you can being to make your planting list. The questions you ask for picking out general plants can be used when choosing food plants.

- Are they healthy plants?
- Which variety of the plant should you choose?
- Are seeds or seedlings better for you?
- Will they thrive in your garden soil and conditions?
- How many plants do you need?
- Do they need special care?

- Where should you position them in the garden?

You also need to know when to plant them. The growing season is very important when you're growing food and you may choose to plant and harvest according to the lunar cycle, an ancient and well regarded system of gardening.

Also make sure that you have checked what conditions the plant requires – the right amount of sun or shade, good drainage or rich soil can make all the difference to the size of your crop.

You can also dowse to check when you are going to harvest your crop. Dowse over the plants to check that they are ready. Which would be the best way to store your crop.

Growing and using herbs

Herbs, especially medicinal herbs are a very good subject for pendulum dowsing. You can dowse the whole process of selecting, buying and growing your herbs as you would for any other plant, but you can also dowse to check that you are choosing the right herb for a specific healing energy.

If you are trying to decide which herb to use for a particular problem, write their names on pieces of paper (taking care to get the species and variety correct) and dowse over each one.

14

Psychic, Energy and Spiritual dowsing.

The dowsing pendulum is a wonderful tool for helping you work with spiritual energy and it can be said that dowsing itself is the use of psychic energy, and a form of divination when used to ask questions about the future.

There are many energies that surround us that are not visible, but that can have a very strong effect on our well-being on all levels, spiritual and emotional, mental and physical.

Energy dowsing

Some people are very sensitive to geographic stress and electromagnetic fields, while others believe that it affects all of us even if we don't accept it.

In our modern world, we are surrounded by electrical energy and magnetic fields that are very unnatural. Many of us suffer from headaches, insomnia, irritability and general ill-health, and we also live our lives surrounded by computers and TVs, mobile phones mobile computers and all sorts of other electrical equipment.

You can dowse to check pieces of equipment to see if specific pieces are causing you a problem. For instance the energy output of a particular mobile phone might be a problem for you, or you could have problems with mobile phones in general, in which case your could try to limit your use of them or see if a bluetooth headset could make it easier for you.

If you feel that there is a place that is uncomfortable for you, work with your dowsing pendulum to check the energy in that area. Ask your pendulum to show you whether the energy is positive or negative. You may find that it is negative or you may find that it is simply incompatible with your personal energy. Whichever it is, once you know, you can do something about it, either avoiding that particular area or being prepared to deal with the energies when you do have to go there.

For instance, there may be one particular supermarket in which you find shopping a nightmare. If you know that the actual ground that the supermarket is built on has negative energy, you can either avoid going to that supermarket altogether or, if that isn't practical, try to make all other parts of the experience positive, avoiding the busiest times, avoiding it altogether if you're stressed or doing some meditation beforehand to give yourself some protection from the negative energy.

Spiritual dowsing

Finding your spiritual path in life is essential to finding happiness and contentment and can be one of the most difficult searches you make. Sometimes the harder you look for the path the more difficult it is to see it.

Working with your dowsing pendulum is an excellent way of refining your thoughts and wishes and discovering what is your true path, rather than the path that logic dictates or others would dictate for you.

The very act of leaning to work with a pendulum is part of your spiritual growth, part of your journey as you open up to spiritual energies and allowing your thirst for knowledge to develop.

Once you have become comfortable with your pendulum, it can be a tool to help you on your journey. Helping you choose the right course, the right teachers, the right books to read, the right area of study.

You may already have some idea of the direction you want to take but feel unsure. You may have been finding reasons to delay your decision or put it off altogether for years. You're too busy, other people and family have to come first, you haven't the time to do it properly, it's just daydreaming. So many people put off their dreams forever and I think that 'I wish I had ....' Is one of the saddest things to hear someone say.

Once you decide to face your fears and work with your pendulum on questions about your spiritual development you should set aside some quality time and prepare yourself properly.

This is a very important and potentially life changing set of questions and decisions. So do not take it on lightly and make sure that your energy is clean and positive that you are in a calm and loving area, and that you think carefully about your questions and phrase them clearly. As always, remember the dowsing pendulum is not a toy and dowsing is not a game.

You should spend time preparing yourself for this session.

Take the time over days or even weeks to think about what your questions should be. You may even prefer to write a list.

You must be calm and emotionally balanced before you start this dowsing session. Having a blazing row with your loved one is not good preparation, and neither is an awful day at work. It might be tempting to ask your dowsing pendulum if you should make a major life change in one of those situations, but your emotions will make any response from the pendulum useless.

Finding your spiritual path may well involve changing the entire pattern of your life. It is a daunting process, and one that many of us will never face. After all, it's much easier to simply go on doing what you're doing even though it is not making you happy, and in many cases making you positively unhappy. But staying in your rut has a certain type of comfort, and it can be terrifying to move out of the rut, no matter how miserable it might be making you.

The questions you might be asking in a session like this are intensely personal, and much more complex than deciding on a new career or which university course to do. In deciding your spiritual path in life you are making much deeper decisions.

Some people leave highly paid professional careers and outwardly successful lifestyles to embark on missionary work in the Third World, to sail around the world on a yacht or start their own gardening business.

Others will leave their high-powered, high-pressure careers to be self-sufficient, miles from the city lives they have been living. While some will find that they have a religious vocation and choose to give up the world to live in a monastery.

Not everyone will feel that they need to make or even ask about these life changing decisions. Many of us have been lucky enough to find the right place in life by following our instincts.

If you do decide that some point that you want to work with your dowsing pendulum on this area, your mental and psychic preparation is even more important than normal.

Make sure that you set aside some quality time for yourself where you will not be disturbed, and you can focus your attention. You could have a relaxing bath, adding herbs or aromatherapy oils to the bathwater to aid your relaxation. A period of meditation will help clear your mind of negative thoughts.

Once you have prepared yourself find a quiet space with calm, positive energy. You can light scented candles or play soothing music if they help you focus and relax.

- Calm your thoughts and empty your mind of negative energies trying to distance yourself from any emotions, you might feel about the question.
- Take a deep breath and let it out slowly.
- Hold the pendulum between the thumb and forefinger letting your wrist relax.
- Ask your pendulum, if it is appropriate to begin this particular line of questioning at this time.

As long as you have received a positive answer to this initial question you can begin to ask your questions.

Dowsing and Divination or Fortune Telling

The terms dowsing and divination are used almost interchangeably by some people, but I feel that this does a disservice to both although the confusion is understandable, because the term 'to divine water ' does mean to discover water by dowsing.

Dowsing whether with rods, or with a pendulum is the art of finding something that is hidden. It can be something that is physical, such as water, archaeology or a specific missing item, or it can be knowledge that is hidden, as in decision-making.

We have touched on divination throughout this book when looking for guidance in decision making, but divination often looks further into the future, with a lot less structure to your question.

According to the Oxford dictionary, divination, is the practice of seeking knowledge of the future, and that is what people normally mean when they talk of divination, whether that is by use of the tarot cards, reading the tea leaves or with the use of dowsing.

Of course, people often refer to it as fortune-telling and although the psychic skills are as old as humanity, in our modern society it has been relegated to the status of a sideshow at the funfair, so much so that respected psychics in the UK are now legally required to state that their readings are given for entertainment purposes only.

The form of divination that most people will have come across with the dowsing pendulum will have been to see someone dowsing over 'the bump' to tell whether the baby will be a boy or girl. This can be done very seriously by an experienced dowser, but also very often it's done as a party trick, which undermines the whole process of divination and dowsing.

Personally I feel you should take great care with any type of divination whether that is with your pendulum or whether you choose to use tarot cards or any of the other ancient methods of divination, and you should understand the process and energies of divination before you introduce pendulum dowsing into this area.

Many people who use a pendulum for divination like to use charts, these are simply diagrams that you have prepared yourself or purchased, that give you a focus for your dowsing. For instance, you can have an alphabet chart which you would use to ask you pendulum to spell out words as with a Ouija board.

Whatever method you choose, remember that you must take the process seriously and you must respect the energies you are working with. As with any divination, the answers are a guide and how you interpret them and act of them is just as important as the answer itself.

Dowsing Psychic energies

Working with a dowsing pendulum or with dowsing rods is a form of working with psychic energy. In this section, I am referring to working with your dowsing pendulum in other areas of psychic work, such as ghost hunting.

Working with your dowsing pendulum on this type of psychic energy is a very specialised area of dowsing and should not be undertaken lightly although unfortunately it often is.

Working with psychic energies and the paranormal or channelling must be taken very seriously in the same way as you should tarot cards or a Ouija board.

You must take great care to protect yourself from negative energies and psychic attack.

You should have some knowledge and experience of working with these energies before you involve your dowsing pendulum.

Ghost hunting has become very popular but it's important to note that the number of exorcisms being carried out has also increased.

When we work with our dowsing pendulum in any area of life we are looking for negatives and positives, often working with the pendulum to find areas of negative or positive energy in the body, in our homes and work or in an area of the country. So the very act of working with a dowsing pendulum means that you do believe in negative as well as positive energy. And it's only a short step to accepting that there are some very negative energies in some areas and these need to be treated with great care and respect.

Novels and films of vampires, werewolves, demons, fairies and ghosts mean that many people have developed a fascination with the paranormal, and a genuine and respectful investigation into the paranormal can be incredible and life changing. Just don't step in blindly and trip over the abyss.

If you do decide to follow this area of dowsing, please research it carefully and find a supportive group of like minded people whose energies you are comfortable with.

15

The Pendulum and relationship questions

I've given this subject its own chapter because romantic questions are one of the most popular areas for pendulum dowsing, both for professional dowsers and for individuals, but is also one where it is most difficult to remain neutral, so take time before you rush for your pendulum after the first date.

Even if you are asking a seemingly straightforward question - is Mr X the right man for me (or of course Miss Y the right woman) the question still has to be phrased exactly - are you looking for a date for the weekend or a lifetime partner?

Remember, you have to be sure that you can stay neutral!

In fact, although partnership questions are sometimes the most popular, and can be the one of the most important, it is also one of the areas in which dowsing is most misused.

Dowsing with your pendulum shouldn't just be a joke or a party trick – you should have much more respect for it than that. And relationships are one of the most complex areas of our lives, so make sure that you have thought seriously about the type of relationship you want – or don't want – before you start to phrase your question.

The answer to the question 'Am I going to marry this person?' may well be no. But if that is the question you ask, you will have no way of telling if you would have had a long and beautiful relationship that was good for both partners but not destined to lead to marriage. Be careful what you ask!

Once you've heeded these warnings, it's worth saying that pendulum dowsing can be extremely successful in the area of personal relationships.

Relationships are the centre of all our lives. Not only romantic relationships, but friends, work colleagues, business partners, neighbours, and of course family.

All of these relationships can become a bit confusing at times and dowsing is a very good way of being able to work your way through a potential problem.

When it comes down to the basics, compatibility is the main force in relationships, and questions about compatibility can be focused very clearly and is something that a pendulum can work on very well.

The actual question will be personal to you and to the situation, but a good place to start is by asking 'are these two people compatible?'

You can begin to narrow it down by specifying the area you are interested in. It might be one, some or all of these areas of compatibility depending on the type of relationship.

- physical compatibility
- mental compatibility
- emotional compatibility
- spiritual compatibility
- financial compatibility
- ethical compatibility

The types of compatibility that matter, will vary with different types of relationship.

In a business relationship, attitudes to finance, risk, work ethic – indeed ethics in general will matter a great deal.

If you're choosing a flatmate, the attitude to paying the bills will still matter, but so will the attitude to the level of tidiness, ownership of the fridge contents and the amount of partying that is acceptable!

Dowsing romantic relationships

Remember – you have to remain neutral to be able to get a clear answer, and you have to be able to remain in a calm environment. So you might find that if you are asking a question for someone else their own emotional intensity will disturb your ability to be able to use your dowsing pendulum to get a clear answer. If that is the case, you will have to ask them if they can calm their emotions. Or possibly, you would have to work with your dowsing pendulum at a later date, without them being present.

Many people will ask you to dowse about the latest subject of their romantic interest without believing that there is any validity in pendulum dowsing in the first place. They will consider it a joke or a party trick.

While healthy scepticism is fine, and you will dowse for many people who have doubts about the ability of the pendulum until they see it working for themselves, it is a little more difficult when people simply consider it in the same light as a magic trick. ' Oh, will Brad Pitt fall in love with me?' is not a serious respectful question.

If you simply treat your dowsing pendulum as a toy you will lose the energy link between you and the pendulum. So don't allow other people to persuade you into playing the games.

Once you know that a person's intention is serious, talk to them for a few minutes so that you can identify what their real questions are. This is best done on a one-to-one basis without any other friends being involved, because the answers are very important and must be honest if you are going to get an accurate reading from your pendulum.

Preparing to Dowse for a Romantic Relationship

Before you start, make sure that you are calm ⌣ surround yourself with positive energies trying to stay neutral and keep your questions very clear.

Sit in a quiet space, with a calm, positive energy. You might want to play some soothing music or light some scented candles

If you're dowsing for yourself, picture the person you are asking about clearly.

If you are dowsing for someone else, form a mental picture of both of the people.

You can also simply write their names on a piece of paper and focus on the papers.

If you're using papers, place them on a clear table in front of you. You could surround them with polished, tumbled Stones of rose quartz, the Love Stone to create a circle of love, self-confidence and self-esteem.

Relax. Calm and empty your mind of any preconceived opinions or emotions, take some deep breaths

Ask the pendulum if it is alright for you to begin your questions. 'Can I ask this question?' 'am I ready?'

As long as you have received the positive indicator for the preparation question, hold the pendulum over the names on the paper and ask your questions

As with all dowsing, the larger and smoother the indicator action, the stronger the answer. If your 'yes' indicator is a clockwise circle, the larger and smoother the circle the stronger the 'yes'.

If your pendulum begins to make very small movements, or erratic movements, it may indicate that you are not maintaining your neutrality or the questions are becoming too unfocused.

If that happens, take a break, calm your mind and try to re-focus your attention. If you can't – then leave the dowsing for a while. You can't force answers and you will simply end up irritated and frustrated. Calm your mind and come back to the question at another time.

Dowsing for a non-romantic relationship

You will probably find that most of your relationship pendulum dowsing will be about romantic relationships. After all, these are the most important to us and the ones that people are most likely to ask you about. But other relationships shouldn't be ignored, although we don't tend to give them the same importance in our minds.

In reality, they can be extremely important to our health and well-being on all levels.

An incompatible business relationship can cause us stress, financial headaches and serious ill health. It can be very difficult to walk away from an unsuccessful business relationship once you are entangled. And this can be true, whether you have gone into business with somebody, or if the problem is with a co-worker or superior.

Obviously it is far better to avoid these problems in the first place. But even if you have become entangled, clarifying what the problem is by asking your dowsing pendulum the right questions can be the first step in knowing how to move on with your life.

The wrong friendship can also cause a great deal of stress and unhappiness. Many people remain friends with another person out of some sense of loyalty, guilt or simply the fact that the other person has an emotional or mental hold on them. This type of friendship, mired in negative emotions as it is, can be very destructive. Clarifying the energies that are involved in such a friendship by asking the right questions of your dowsing pendulum can help you see the situation clearly and give you the energy and impetus to move on.

There are also many of us looking for flatmates or housemates at the moment. After all, housing costs are extremely high and sometimes sharing is the only way that we can get onto the housing ladder. Of course, many people's first experience of living away from home can be moving to university and flat sharing that is part of that experience.

The new home and new friends should be the beginning of an exciting new period in your life. So it's important that you choose the right people to share that with, and your dowsing pendulum can be an invaluable tool in making those choices. There are bound to be tensions between any group of people, but some of them are more serious than normal and these are the ones that you want to avoid. That very often means avoiding the problem of including the one person who can create tension at all times. Unfortunately they can be very difficult to spot. It isn't always the obvious, possibly argumentative person that is really the problem. It can be the quite 'peacemaker' that is really stirring everyone else up, mixing the pot and then sitting back!

Obviously, these different types of relationships come with different questions. Compatibility is still at the heart of any question, but the emphasis and the time span will be different in different types of relationships.

Finding the right flatmates for university is a question for one or two years, although you may well make friendships that will last a lifetime. But your priorities will be different, if you are planning on starting a business with someone.

Once you have thought seriously about what the relationship is and what you need out of it, you will be able to clarify your questions.

For instance, if you are starting a business, do you see the future as building up the business and selling it on for a profit in four or five years? Or do you see it as a lifetime commitment? It's important that business partners are on the same track.

Before you start, make sure that you are calm and surround yourself with positive energies trying to stay neutral and keep your questions very clear.

Sit in a quiet space, with a calm, positive energy. You might want to play some soothing music or light some scented candles

Sits comfortably and don't cross your legs, you don't want to enclose your energy.

Relax. Calm and empty your mind of any preconceived opinions or emotions, take some deep breaths

Once you have identified your question, write the names of the people a clean piece of paper. If you are checking the best compatibility of a number of people – for instance, potential flatmates - write each name onto separate pieces of paper so that you can move them into proximity with each other separately.

Place the papers on a clear table in front of you – don't allow other clutter to get in the way.

Ask the pendulum if it is alright for you to begin your questions. 'Can I ask this question?' 'am I ready?'

As long as you have received the positive indicator for the preparation question, hold the pendulum over the names on the paper and ask your questions

If you're dowsing about a group of people - for instance flatmates - there will be one central person. Either yourself or the person you are asking the question for. After all, there's no point finding a perfect combination of people that excludes you (or your questioner)!

Place your name (or your questioner) in the centre of the table with the other potential names, surrounding it.

Focusing on your question, hold your dowsing pendulum over one of the names and make a note of the response, including how strong it is.

Continue this process over the each of the names until you have an answer for each person.

If you have been using the dowsing process to narrow a list of names. You can then select the names you have received the strongest positive response to and group them together.

Refocus your question, and dowse over the group of names as a whole.

Obviously, you will need to adapt your questions and method of pendulum dowsing to suit the specific nature of the relationship you are working on and the questions you are seeking answers to.

16

Dowsing for what is lost

Pendulum Dowsing can be a very powerful tool in searching for something that is lost. You can use your pendulum to find things such as keys and jewellery, or even lost pets. There are some dowsing experts who dowse for missing people, but this is not a task to be undertaken lightly, as it is fraught with difficult emotions and energies.

However, most of the time, you don't have to worry about emotional   trauma, when you're dowsing for something that is lost, as in most cases it is simply frustrating when you misplace something simple, your keys, a book, a piece of jewellery - anything really. There are some days when I feel I could lose anything that is not physically attached!

When you are dowsing for something you've misplaced, and you have an idea of the general area, such as your office or your home, the dowsing is a little like playing the hot and cold game again.

Focus your mind clearly on the item you are looking for. If you're looking for car keys, focus on which car and the fact that you want the keys that you use every day. Otherwise, you might find the keys to the house or the spare keys for the car that you keep safely in the drawer, but they don't have the house keys attached to them.

Making sure you stay focused on exactly what you are looking for (the Garnet earrings, not pearl earrings) will save you the frustration of finding something you were not looking for.

If you are searching in a very localised area – for instance inside the house – simply ask your pendulum directional questions.

You can do this by using a form of the children's game of getting hotter/getting colder.

Start by clearly visualising the item you have lost – picture the piece of jewellery, really focus on what type of keys, or exactly what the missing credit card receipt was for.

Dowse mentally from room to room

- Are the everyday car keys to the Ford in the kitchen?
- Are the everyday car keys to the Ford in the master bedroom?
- Are the everyday car keys to the Ford in the hall way?

Work your way mentally through the different rooms in your home until your pendulum gives you the 'yes' indicator. You can physically move to each room as you ask if you prefer

Once your pendulum has indicated the correct room you can actually enter that space and move slowly around it, asking your pendulum to indicate when you are getting closer to the item.

The 'yes' indicator will grow stronger as you close in, and it will begin to weaken if you move past the hot spot. Move more slowly and deliberately if the object is very small – it would be easier to miss the right spot.

If you are working in a wider area you will need a different approach. It simply isn't practical to visit every part of a larger search area so you need help in narrowing down the possibilities.

A chart such as the one below, can be very helpful as a direction finder when you are dowsing for lost items on a bigger scale.

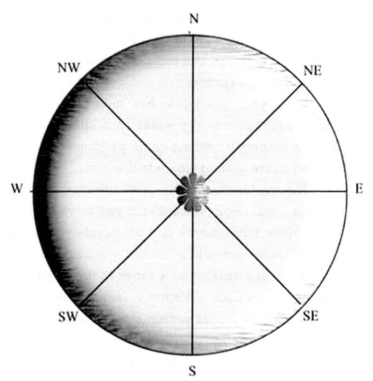

Using a simple direction finder like this means that you can work anywhere and together with your compass, the chart can help you stay on track, clearly showing you when you need to change direction.

First of all be very clear what you are looking for. Again, 'find my keys', is no good as a question because you haven't specified which keys! You may find it helps to ask your question out loud rather than just thinking it, and visualise the item you are searching for as you focus your attention.

If you are searching for a lost pet, you can hold something belonging to the pet or a piece of the missing pets fur to help you focus

Make sure that you have lined up your chart to north – use your compass.

Ask the pendulum which direction you should begin your search in, by dowsing over each direction in turn until you get a 'yes', starting at north and moving clockwise. Once you reach the right direction on your chart you will get your 'yes' indicator.

Move off in that direction, still working with your pendulum. When the pendulum stops giving your 'yes' indicator, or it begins to weaken, stop, realign your chart to the north with your compass, then ask again.

You can also work with a map of the area, or preferably a series of maps, starting with a map of the wider area and working down towards more detailed maps as you have narrowed the search area.

Although it is quite easy to search for lost items, the more intense the emotional energy, the more difficult the task, and it is very important to remain calm and neutral when dowsing even though it can be very difficult.

If you are dowsing for a lost animal, ask your pendulum to take you to the animal. You are asking for the place where you will meet, rather than the place that the animal actually is at the time you ask the question. Otherwise you could spend a great deal of time chasing after where the animal has been.

Use the techniques described above for working with the directional finder.

Once you reach the area that the pendulum has guided you to, have patience. A scared animal will hide in the most unlikely places and needs to be able to relax enough to come to you.

You have to make your own decision as to how long you search for a lost pet. It is a very difficult emotional time and you may 'feel' that you should keep looking long after people have told you to give up.

One of my cats – a real character – decided to walk out in a huff, literally! Someone laughed at him and he stormed off! After a week, everyone told me to give up, but I 'knew' he was still out there, so I kept searching and he was brought back kicking and screaming – again literally – after almost three weeks. Many years later he did meet with an accident, and I 'knew' he was gone straight away. One of the side-effects of working with the dowsing pendulum is it you will become more sensitive and more able to listen to your instincts.

Dowsing for a missing person

Dowsing for a missing person is even more fraught with many very negative emotions and should only be undertaken by very experienced dowsers who will approach the task with great caution. It may seem like a good idea to try and help a family in great distress, but you should be very, very careful before you even think of becoming involved in this area. There may be physical dangers in such a search, as well as emotional, mental and psychic risks. If you feel drawn to this type of dowsing, find an organisation that you are comfortable with, so that you have the support of others.

Dowsing and archaeology

We tend to think of a metal detector being a tool of choice for amateur archaeologists but in fact, dowsing has been a very popular tool with some archaeologists for many years, although understandably many are reluctant to admit it.

After all, dowsing with a pendulum or rods is done in many cases to find things that are hidden from view, whether that is water or minerals or something we've lost. So it makes sense that you can also dowse for archaeology that is hidden beneath the ground.

There are many examples over the years of dowsing being used with archaeology.

For instance, the Roman bathhouse at Beaumont Park, whose location was discovered by Gerald Brodridd, was initially pinpointed while he was looking for evidence of Roman occupation with his dowsing rods, and of course, with the permission of the landowner.

The British Society of Dowsers has an archaeological dowsing group, and they keep detailed records of their work. As with many types of dowsing, the search can be carried out either on site or over a map of the area. You may be asking your dowsing pendulum to find something precise, but with archaeology it's more likely that you will be asking it to find a place to start the investigation or begin digging a trench. So your question would be more general than normal with dowsing.

Of course, you should follow the same rules as with a metal detector or any other method of archaeology - do not go digging up someone's field without permission! And as with all archaeology, the context of a find is vitally important, so it is always much better if you work with a group. If you would like further information on this fascinating area of dowsing contact the British Society of Dowsers in London or check their website.

Map Dowsing

Map dowsing is similar in some ways to dowsing for lost items. In fact, you can use it to dowse for objects or animals that are lost in a wider area. But map dowsing can also be used for any type of searching.

In fact, I have mentioned map dowsing a number of times in previous chapters, it can be used in many situations, whether you're searching for a new home, an archaeological site or something you've lost. The American dowser Verne Cameron worked with map dowsing when he pinpointed the position of American and Soviet nuclear submarines in the Pacific.

In order to give you and your pendulum the best opportunity to succeed, you must work with the most accurate and largest scale map that is possible.

Start as you always do, by focusing on exactly what you want to find. For instance, if you were looking for water - are you looking for a usable supply of safe drinking water rather than contaminated or salt water?

If you are looking for metal, are you searching for ancient Roman coins or a source of precious metal that can be mined economically?

This is always the most vital stage of dowsing – you must focus clearly on exactly what it is you are trying to find.

Preparing to Map Dowse

Once you have clearly focused on the item, substance or object you wish to find, clear and calm your mind.

Place the map flat in a clear, uncluttered area. If you are using a table – clear it rather than just edging other items to one side.

Sit comfortably and don't cross your legs, you don't want to enclose your energy

Relax. Calm and empty your mind of any preconceived opinions or emotions, take some deep breaths

Ask the pendulum if it is alright for you to begin your questions. 'Can I ask this question?' 'am I ready?'

As long as you have received the positive indicator for the preparation question, hold the pendulum over the map and ask your questions

Using the map

Start at one side or corner of the map and ask your pendulum if the item is in that direction or in that area.

Repeat this across the map until you receive a positive response.

At this stage you may have to move to a more detailed map that concentrates on the area identified.

Continue in this way until you have identified a specific area.

This may lead you directly to the item you are dowsing for, or you may need to do a detailed, on the spot search.

Map dowsing becomes easier with practice and it is a method used by many professional dowsers and dowsing experts, including those employed by governments and large companies.

Many expert dowsers don't even need to visit the country that they are dowsing for, they can do the search in the comfort of their own home and send the map co-ordinates to those who will actually make the physical search.

19

And into the future

Once you have become comfortable with your pendulum, the future is up to you.

Use the pendulum in areas that you feel comfortable with. Many people specialise with their dowsing. This book covers a wide range of areas and applications but I'm not suggesting that everyone will work with the pendulum in every area of life.

You may have picked up this book because you're interested in a very specific area, you may already work with Reiki energy or crystals for healing and want to introduce dowsing to your healing work. Or you may have seen someone working with the pendulum and wanted to know more about it.

Whatever drew you to dowsing, I hope I have introduced you to some more areas where you can work with your dowsing pendulum and that you will enjoy your journey into this fascinating world.

Practice and work with your pendulum regularly - you will become more in tune with it, the more often you use it. Carry it with you, and once it is tuned into you, don't let other people use it.

Enjoy your dowsing!

About the Author

From a long line of healers on the West Coast of Ireland, Brenda has worked with a dowsing pendulum and healing crystals for over 15 years and is a member of the British Society of Dowsers.

She regularly gives talks and classes on dowsing, vibrational therapies, crystal healing and colour healing as well as writing books, articles and well known series of Core Information charts on a number of alternative therapies.

you can contact her at:
brenda@healing-earth.co.uk
website: www.healing earth.co.uk

Made in the USA
Middletown, DE
03 October 2020